C000157655

A pause
and a prayer

down-to-earth prayers
for daily life

**kevin
mayhew**

First published in 2006 by

KEVIN MAYHEW LTD
Buxhall, Stowmarket, Suffolk, IP14 3BW
E-mail: info@kevinmayhewltd.com
Website: www.kevinmayhew.com

9 8 7 6 5 4 3 2 1 0

ISBN 1 84417 522 7
Catalogue No. 1500877

Designed by Chris Coe

Printed and bound in China

Contents

Introduction

Care from the cradle to the grave – it's what every one of us would like to think we'll receive, however long or short our life may prove to be, and in the UK at least we're lucky enough to have just that provided by the NHS and welfare state. Yes, these may be imperfect, a few people slipping through the net altogether, but most of us can be assured of help and support should we need it through every stage of life. Inevitably, though, such care is limited, largely confined to meeting our physical needs. What, then, of our deeper yearnings, the spiritual void we long to fill? What does faith have to say about the wider journey of life?

In this book, through a selection of material taken from three of my recent publications, I offer prayers inspired by some of the milestones we encounter during that journey – from birth to adulthood, marriage to a new home, middle years to old age – exploring some of the joys, sorrows, temptations and decisions each of these bring, but above all asking how they might speak to us of God. Faith, of course, cannot offer any immunity from life's trials, these being as real for the Christian as any. What it does offer is strength, guidance, comfort and inspiration in abundance; the knowledge that God is with us throughout the journey, and beyond, able to offer care not just from the cradle to the grave but for all eternity.

Nick Fawcett

The baby

I held her, Lord,
  that tiny life,
  so vulnerable and dependent
  yet so full of promise,
  cradled in my arms.
Who could say what the future might hold,
  what adventures and achievements might lie ahead?
Life was a blank canvas,
  the details yet to be sketched.

Lord, for me such freshness is a distant memory,
  the portrait of my life all but drawn,
  days as much about memories as anticipation,
  about what **was** as what yet might be.
Yet that is to forget the fresh start you daily make possible.
Rekindle in me the flame of hope
  and fire of expectancy,
  in the knowledge that, with you,
  however old we might be,
  life has always only just begun.

Amen.

The toddler

He was into everything —
  impatient,
  inquisitive,
  incorrigible —
  and though he needed the occasional restraining hand,
  I'd have had it no other way.
He was eager to explore,
  thirsting for knowledge,
  conscious of so much still to be discovered and understood.

Lord, give me that same desire in terms of faith —
  a resolve to grow in commitment,
  develop in understanding
  and mature in discipleship.
Keep me young in spirit,
  childlike in my appetite for life
  and ever-youthful in my hunger to learn more of the world
  and more of you.

Amen.

The nightlight

It gave just a glow,
   no more,
   but it was enough to dispel the gloom
   and, with it, the child's fear,
   bringing a sense of security,
   welcome reassurance during the dark hours of the night.

Help me, Lord, to glimpse **your** light
   even when life is at its darkest.
Though the night of sorrow, fear, pain or doubt closes in,
   cold and forbidding,
   may a glimmer of your love shine through —
   a glimpse of your presence sufficient to sustain faith,
   nourish hope
   and impart peace.

Amen.

The children's slide

They ran eagerly into the playground,
   bounding up the steps to the top of the slide
   and screaming with delight as they hurtled down it.
But then one slid faster than the rest,
   careering off the end and crashing onto the tarmac,
   where he lay, bruised and shaken.
There were tears for a moment,
   but not for long ...
   almost immediately he was climbing again,
   enthusiasm undiminished,
   such tumbles a price worth paying.

Sometimes, Lord, life brings **me** down to earth with a bump –
   dreams shattered, plans frustrated, happiness destroyed.
Help me at such times,
   instead of feeling sorry for myself
   and cursing my luck,
   to pick myself up and start again,
   knowing that there is no gain without pain,
   no joy without sorrow,
   no laughter without tears.
However often I may fall,
   renew my trust in life
   and in you.

Amen.

The medicine

She gulped it down hurriedly,
  screwing up her face in disgust,
  the taste far from her liking,
  but she knew it was needed,
  vital if she was to get well,
  so she opened her mouth again,
  reluctant but dutiful,
  and accepted the full dose.

Lord, you ask me sometimes to take **my** medicine,
  unwelcome though it might be:
  to face up to the consequences of my actions,
  pay the price of some folly,
  swallow my pride,
  learn my lesson,
  pay my dues.
I don't enjoy it any more than the next person,
  but help me at such times to remember it's for my own good,
  the prescription designed to heal, not hurt,
  correct rather than castigate,
  discipline instead of punish.
Though I do not relish the treatment,
  use it to make me whole.

Amen.

The toyshop

It was awash with delights . . .
  or at least it was for the children,
  their eyes round with wonder,
  fingers unable to resist picking up now this, now that —
  the range of toys and games so vast it was hard for them
  to choose.
And it would have been the same once for me,
  the time being when I too
  would have felt similar excitement at such a sight.
Only, of course, childhood had passed,
  and I'd moved on,
  such pursuits long since left behind.

Have I moved on in **faith**, Lord,
  there, too, leaving former ways behind,
  or do I **play** at discipleship,
  treating it as a game instead of being serious about commitment?
Have I matured as a person,
  growing up not only as an individual
  but also in my dealings with others,
  or do I still lack maturity,
  even being infantile sometimes in my behaviour?
Teach me to be childlike in attitude but not childish,
  to display the trust, innocence and enthusiasm of youth,
  yet also the wisdom, sensitivity and understanding of later years.

Amen.

The school

They filed through the doors,
  some eagerly,
  some dragging their heels;
  many academically able,
  others with different gifts,
  but whatever their abilities,
  each would learn something that day –
  each discover more about themselves and the world
  around them.

Teach me more of **you**, Lord,
  and instruct me in your ways.
Open my heart and mind to your guidance,
  and give me a receptive spirit,
  that I may learn to know you better,
  grasping more of your will
  and growing in faith and understanding.
Remind me that, however much I have fathomed of your purpose
  or experienced of your love,
  there is more still to discover,
  more than I can ever hope to comprehend.

Amen.

The teenager

A difficult age, they called it,
   and so it was,
   not just for his parents but for him as well:
   a time for finding his feet and developing his own identity,
   and inevitably that involved rebellion at times,
   reacting against received wisdom and challenging the status quo
   until he'd worked out for himself where he stood and why.

Teach me, Lord, that rebellion has a place in **discipleship** too:
   that genuine commitment sometimes means questioning
   the ways of the world,
   and being ready, where necessary, to protest against
   accepted norms,
   confronting wrongs and combatting evil,
   however unpopular that may make me.
Though I mellow with the years,
   keep alive the defiance of youth
   when it comes to standing up for you.

Amen.

The exam paper

It was a tough paper, no doubt about that,
   so I was pleased not just to pass
   but to pass well.
Yet if two-thirds of the answers were right,
   a third also were wrong,
   much understood
   but plenty more beyond me.

For some reason, Lord, questions about you are discouraged,
   as though we either shouldn't have any
   or should know all the answers.
Yet if, even in small things, I have gaps in my knowledge,
   how much more so must it be when it comes to you?
Teach me, recognising your greatness
   and the limitations of my understanding,
   to ask honestly and openly about matters of faith,
   conscious that, however much I have grasped,
   there is always far more still to learn.

Amen.

The ecstasy tablet

They looked harmless enough,
   more like sweets than a drug,
   and though they cost rather more
   they were being handed out like Smarties.
Let your hair down, was the message:
   relax . . . live a little.
Why not? Everyone else is.
But as they stumbled home, the cold light of day returning,
   how many spared a thought for the girl in intensive care,
   poisoned by the adulterated tablet;
   the pensioner mugged of her savings to pay for the
   growing addiction;
   the youngsters moving on to crack cocaine;
   the hallucinating child,
   the boy waking up to black depression,
   or the teenager thrown into a fit?

Reach out, Lord, to all who,
   seeking freedom and fulfilment,
   abuse their bodies to escape them;
   all who, in their search for happiness,
   are vulnerable to unscrupulous predators.
Help them to get a buzz out of life not through chemically
   induced elation
   but through experiencing the thrill of your presence
   and tasting the inner ecstasy that you alone can bring.

Amen.

The wedding ring

It was nothing fancy,
  just an ordinary ring,
  worth little in monetary terms,
  but in terms of the reality it represented, priceless,
  speaking of a love that had stood the test of time —
  of an ongoing relationship,
  enduring commitment
  and bond that would not be broken.

Thank you, Lord, for the relationship I enjoy with you —
  your faithfulness across the years,
  your enduring love,
  your companionship through the journey of life —
  and forgive me that all too often it has been one-sided,
  you having to do all the running.
Renew my commitment and deepen my devotion,
  so that I may respond in kind,
  offering something back to you
  who have given so much for me.

Amen.

The new home

It was an unsettling few months —
   weighing up the pros and cons, checking the bank balance,
   viewing properties, packing belongings —
   but at last it was done:
   contracts exchanged and keys handed over.
Yet they still had their doubts,
   on the one hand, excited,
   on the other, fearful.
Would the neighbours be OK, the roof leak,
   the double-glazing need replacing?
Would the policy cover the mortgage,
   interest rates stay low,
   the market keep on rising?
Time alone would tell.

Lord, you promise us another home,
   not made with human hands but kept in heaven,
   a house with many rooms,
   where we will dwell in the light of your love for evermore.
I'm not sure of the details —
   where or when it will be, or what form life will take there —
   but that's not important, for you tell me all I need to know.
Time indeed **will** tell.

Amen.

The removal van

It came as a shock:
  box upon box,
  crate after crate,
  a mountain of possessions I barely knew I had.
They'd built up over the years —
  stuffed into cupboards,
  stashed into drawers,
  or simply piled high in the shed, loft, garage —
  and though I'd had the occasional sift through,
  they'd accumulated faster than I could dispose of them,
  until they filled almost every nook and cranny.

Lord, I mean to focus on treasures in heaven,
  but the lure of earthly goods is so strong
  that I buy first this, then that,
  until the shelves groan and cupboards creak under their weight,
  and the irony, Lord, is that they hang heavy on me too,
  becoming a burden rather than a blessing,
  encumbrance rather than asset.
Teach me to let go of the clutter that ties me to earth,
  so that my spirit might soar unfettered —
  truly free.

Amen.

The salary cheque

It didn't seem much —
  scant reward for another month of toil —
  barely enough to cover the mortgage repayments,
  let alone feed the family, pay the bills
  and have a bit left over for a rainy day.
But what made it worse was knowing that others worked
  no harder
  yet earned far more,
  able to enjoy luxuries I could only dream of,
  to savour a lifestyle that would be always beyond my reach.

It doesn't seem much —
  poor reward indeed for another month of toil —
  but for countless millions it's a fortune,
  enough and more than enough to meet their needs,
  and pay for luxuries undreamt of —
  a square meal, fresh water,
  education and medicine, a roof over their heads.

Remind me, Lord, when I feel hard done by,
  of all I've received,
  the many reasons I have to be thankful.
Instead of envying those with more,
  teach me to remember those with so much less,
  and gratefully to share from my plenty.

Amen.

The insurance policies

They didn't come cheap,
   but they meant I was covered,
   a policy for the house, car, health and mortgage,
   and just about everything else.
Expensive, true,
   but at least I could relax,
   for I was secure, surely —
   protected against whatever vagaries life might bring.

Only of course I wasn't, Lord, was I,
   for there's no telling what tomorrow might bring,
   and however much I try to safeguard earthly possessions,
   they can be plucked from me so swiftly,
   this mortal span like a passing shadow
   and my hold on this world tenuous at best.
Yes, I must look after my loved ones,
   ensuring their security as best I can,
   but remind me of what really counts,
   of the true and lasting treasures found in you alone,
   and teach me to prize those above all else,
   knowing that you are able to keep them safe
   not just now but for all eternity.

Amen.

The benefit office

The numbers flashed up on the screen,
  summoning 'clients' to the appropriate booth,
  and obediently they responded,
  their forms processed,
  their claims dealt with.
Only they weren't numbers;
  they were people,
  with joys, sorrows, hopes and fears,
  just like me.

Reach out, Lord, to the people behind the statistics:
  the mother whose partner has walked out on her and
  the children,
  the worker whose factory has closed down,
  the trader whose business has folded,
  the victim of the industrial accident,
  the manager made redundant,
  the casual labourer whose services are no longer required.
However hopeless they may feel,
  however disheartened, disillusioned or despondent,
  assure them of their worth as individuals,
  and help us as a society to do the same.

Amen.

The cul-de-sac

There'd been no sign,
   no warning —
   one moment it was like any other street
   and the next it just petered out:
   a dead end,
   a road to nowhere.

Lord,
   my life feels like that sometimes.
I stride out confidently,
   believing I know the best way forward,
   only to be pulled up short,
   stopped in my tracks
   by some disappointment, upset, problem or tragedy,
   and I'm left asking, 'What now?'
   'Why am I here?'
   'Where next?'

Speak to me, Lord,
   when life seems bereft of meaning and purpose.
Direct my steps,
   give light to my path
   and lead me in your eternal way.

Amen.

The adult learning centre

They were a good age, some of them —
   fifty,
   sixty,
   even seventy —
   but they weren't afraid to admit the gaps in their knowledge,
   nor to do something about them,
   each more than ready to apply themselves to study:
   to listen and learn.

Forgive me, Lord,
   for I've become complacent,
   assuming I've grasped all I need to know,
   no longer a novice at discipleship but a graduate,
   my education complete.
Teach me that, for all my years of faith,
   there is more still to be learned,
   much that I've barely begun to explore.
Instruct me, then, in your ways,
   and lead me to ever-deeper understanding.

Amen.

The stopwatch

They were racing against the clock,
   every millisecond counting,
   so the athletes strained forward,
   limbs pumping,
   lungs bursting,
   determined to set a new fastest time.

The older I get, Lord, the more life feels like that,
   as though the stopwatch is running and time is running **out**,
   so I rush around from one thing to the next,
   determined to cram ever more into the unforgiving minute.
Yet so easily, in my haste, I forget to enjoy what I have,
   to let go of striving and simply to live.
Remind me that though this mortal span may be slipping away,
   it is just a taste of things to come;
   that though the days are passing I have no cause to fret,
   for with you I have all the time in the world . . .
   and far, far beyond!

Amen.

The GP's waiting room

Why are they here, Lord?
A bad back, perhaps,
   heavy cold,
   twisted muscle?
A bout of indigestion or hacking cough?
Or perhaps something worse,
   more pressing.
An unexplained lump discovered that morning,
   sending an icy chill down the spine?
A diagnosis anxiously awaited,
   spelling relief or panic,
   acquittal or sentence?
A failed pregnancy,
   dreams dashed again?
Calm expressions and averted eyes belie the maelstrom beneath,
   each story locked away until, one by one, names are called,
   and, like penitents at confession,
   they enter the sanctum and blurt out all,
   craving absolution.

Lord, for those troubled about their health,
   and those with the responsibility of ministering to them,
   grant your help, guidance and love.

Amen.

The hospital

I walked through the maze of corridors,
  searching for the right ward,
  and behind the stark labels that greeted me —
  oncology department, men's surgical, maternity suite, mortuary —
  lay a labyrinth of emotions,
  untold individuals waiting and wondering,
  living and dying:
  such hopes . . . yet such fears,
  such joy . . . yet such sorrow,
  such relief . . . yet such pain,
  such healing . . . yet such brokenness —
  a poignant tapestry of delight and despair.

Hear my prayer, Lord, for patients and their loved ones,
  but, above all, for those who staff our hospitals —
  those with the courage to face, day after day, the sheer
  intensity of it all,
  striving with such dedication to nurture wholeness in body,
  mind and spirit.
Thank you for their skill and compassion,
  the renewal they bring,
  life make possible,
  understanding show
  and comfort extend.
Thank you for their willingness to care.

Amen.

The Botox injection

'No more wrinkles,' it said.
'Roll back the years!'
And there was no denying she looked good,
    her skin smoother and firmer than it had been before.
But did she **feel** different – that was the question –
    not just more confident in her appearance,
    but fitter,
    younger,
    energised within?
She could change the outside,
    but what of the rest:
    the attitudes and ideas that shaped her life,
    making her the person she was?

Lord, I don't like growing older any more than the next person,
    but though I can disguise the signs of ageing,
    I can never deny them,
    for they are more than skin deep.
Teach me, as **you** do, to accept who I am,
    and to place into your hands everything I yet might be,
    recognising that you alone are able to bring true renewal,
    not just outwardly
    but deep within.

Amen.

The pensioner

She looked old and wizened,
   her hair white,
   skin wrinkled and paper thin,
   and youngsters passed her by as if she wasn't there,
   but though the flesh sagged, the spirit still sparkled,
   a youthful zest for life belying the frail exterior.

Give me, Lord, the maturity of age
   yet freshness of youth,
   the wisdom of experience
   yet innocence of childhood.
However many my years of faith,
   may my love for you
   and desire to know you better
   be as vibrant as the day they were born,
   the life you have put within me, ever old
   yet ever new.

Amen.

The hearing aid

It changed her life,
   what had been a blur suddenly clear,
   opening up again not just conversation
   but delight in the song of birds,
   the sound of music,
   the splash of waves
   and the laughter of children —
   a world of senses that had long been closed.

Help **me** to hear, Lord,
   not with my ears but with my heart —
   to hear your voice in those around me,
   your word in prayer and worship,
   your call in the daily routine,
   your speech in the miracle of life.
Remind me of the many ways you speak,
   and give me a receptive spirit to hear what you are saying.

Amen.

The photograph album

It had a melancholy feel,
  the dog-eared pages and faded photographs speaking of
  moments long gone,
  past glories and pleasures, for ever plucked away.
But for the pensioner poring over her album
  it was more than an epitaph to distant memories;
  it was a living testimony to special times shared,
  precious people loved,
  and countless experiences enjoyed.

I too, Lord, carry my memories with me,
  if not on paper then in my heart —
  so much I have done,
  so many I have known,
  innumerable people, places, sights and sounds
  that have enriched and enthralled,
  fashioning the person I am today.
For all I have so richly received,
  Lord, thank you.

Amen.

The twilight

The light was fading but not yet gone,
    suffusing the air with a kind of magic
    as life everywhere readied itself for slumber —
    the bustle of the morning long past
    and heat of the day forgotten
    as the chill of night descended,
    precursor to another day.

It set me thinking, Lord, of those in their twilight years,
    the sun beginning to set yet still golden.
Though the energy of youth is long past
    and aspirations of middle years seem distant,
    may this time of life bring joys of its own:
    an inner tranquillity and contentment
    in the light of all that has gone before,
    coupled with confident trust in what is yet to come —
    the new dawn that, by your grace,
    will surely follow the night.

Amen.

The birthday card

It was greeted with excitement,
    hastily torn open in anticipation of a gift inside —
    yet another birthday surprise.

It was greeted with pride,
    for it represented a coming of age,
    a personal milestone,
    the start of a new and exciting chapter.

It was greeted with resignation,
    for it meant another year gone by,
    another year older —
    too much of life gone,
    too little yet to come.

Whatever my stage of life, Lord,
    help me to greet it thankfully,
    knowing that as you have blessed me,
    so you will bless me again,
    each moment given by you,
    and with the best yet to come.

Amen.